## Graceful Beginnings

### Short and Easy for Anyone New to the Bible

# The God You Can Know

*The Wonderful Attributes of Your Father God*

## MELANIE NEWTON

JOYFUL
WALK
BIBLE
STUDIES

*The God You Can Know: The Wonderful Attributes of Your Father God*

© 2025 by Melanie Newton. All rights reserved.

Published by Joyful Walk Press. Flower Mound, TX.

ISBN: 979-8-9926517-4-4

For questions about the use of this study guide or for bulk orders, please email us at melanienewton.com/contact.

Cover photo "Daddy's Little Girl" by Holly, accessed on Flickr.com, used by permission.

Melanie Newton is the author of "Graceful Beginnings" books for anyone new to the Bible and "Joyful Walk Bible Studies" for established Christians. Her mission is to help women learn to study the Bible for themselves and to grow their Bible-teaching skills to lead others.

*Joyful Walk Bible Studies* are grace-based studies for women of all ages. Each study guide follows the inductive method of Bible study (observation, interpretation, application) in a warm and inviting format.

We pray that you will find *The God You Can Know* to be a resource that God will use to strengthen you in your faith walk with Him.

Christ-Focused • Grace-Based • Bible-Rich

JOYFUL WALK PRESS
Flower Mound, TX

## MELANIE NEWTON

Melanie Newton is a Louisiana girl who made the choice to follow Jesus while attending LSU. She and her husband Ron married and moved to Texas for him to attend Dallas Theological Seminary. They stayed in Texas where Ron led a wilderness camping ministry for troubled youth for many years. He now helps corporations with their challenging employees. Melanie jumped into raising three Texas-born children and serving in ministry to women at her church.

Through the years, the Lord has given her opportunity to do Bible teaching and to write grace-based Bible studies for women that are now available from her website (melanienewton.com) and on Bible.org.

Melanie Newton loves to help women learn how to study the Bible for themselves. She also teaches online courses for women to grow their Bible-teaching skills to help others—all with the goal of getting to know Jesus more along the way. Her heart's desire is to encourage you to have a joyful relationship with Jesus Christ so you are willing to share that experience with others around you.

"Jesus took hold of me in 1972, and I've been on this great adventure ever since. My life is a gift of God, full of blessings in the midst of difficult challenges. The more I've learned and experienced God's absolutely amazing grace, the more I've discovered my faith walk to be a joyful one. I'm still seeking that joyful walk every day..."

*Melanie*

# OTHER BIBLE STUDIES BY MELANIE NEWTON

## Graceful Beginnings Series books for anyone new to the Bible:

A Fresh Start (basics for new Christians)
Painting the Portrait of Jesus (the Gospel of John)
The God You Can Know (the character of God)
Grace Overflowing (an overview of Paul's 13 letters)
The Walk from Fear to Faith (7 Old Testament women)
Satisfied by His Love (women who knew Jesus)
Seek the Treasure (study of Ephesians)
Pathways to a Joyful Walk (6 pathways to a joy-filled life)s

## Joyful Walk Bible Studies for growing Christians:

Adorn Yourself with Godliness (1 Timothy and Titus +Spanish)
Everyday Women, Ever Faithful God (Old Testament women +Spanish)
Connecting Faith to Life on Planet Earth (Genesis 1-11; Revelation)
Graceful Living (the essentials for a grace-based Christian life)
Graceful Living Today (a devotional journal for a joyful life)
Healthy Living (Colossians and Philemon)
Heartbreak to Hope (the Gospel of Mark)
Identity: Sticking to Your Faith in a Pull-Apart World (Ezra - Malachi)
Knowing Jesus, Knowing Joy (Philippians +Spanish)
Live Out His Love (New Testament women)
Perspective (1and 2 Thessalonians)
Profiles of Perseverance (Old Testament men +Spanish)
Radical Acts (Acts)
Reboot, Renew, Rejoice (1 and 2 Chronicles)
The God-Dependent Woman (2 Corinthians)
To Be Found Faithful (2 Timothy)

## Resources for leading others

Be a Christ-Focused Small Group Leader
Leap into Lifestyle Disciplemaking
Painting the Picture of Jesus (the "I Am's" of Jesus lessons)
Teaching Children the God They Can Know (the character of God)

Download our catalogue and get resources for your spiritual growth at
melanienewton.com.

# Contents

# Introduction

## GRACEFUL BEGINNINGS

The *Graceful Beginnings* books are Bible studies specifically designed for anyone new to the Bible—whether you are a new Christian or you just feel insecure about understanding the Bible. The short and easy lessons will introduce you to your God and His way of approaching life in simple terms that can be easily understood.

Just as a newborn baby needs to know the love and trustworthiness of her parents, the new Christian needs to know and experience the love and trustworthiness of her God. *A Fresh Start* is the first book in the series, laying a good foundation of truth for you to grasp and apply to your life. The other books in the series can be done in any order.

## SOME BIBLE BASICS

Throughout these lessons, you will use a Bible to answer questions as you discover treasure about your life with Christ. The Bible is one book containing a collection of 66 books combined together for our benefit. It is divided into two main parts: the Old Testament and the New Testament.

The Old Testament tells the story of the beginning of the world and God's promises to mankind given through the nation of Israel. It tells how the people of Israel obeyed and disobeyed God over many, many years. All the stories and messages in the Old Testament lead up to Jesus Christ's coming to the earth.

The New Testament tells the story of Jesus Christ, the early Christians, and God's promises to all those who believe in Jesus. You can think of the Old Testament as "before Christ" and the New Testament as "after Christ."

Each book of the Bible is divided into chapters and verses within those chapters to make it easier to study. Bible references include the book name, chapter number and verse number(s). For example, Ephesians 2:8 refers to the New Testament book of Ephesians, the 2nd chapter, and verse 8 within that 2nd chapter. Printed Bibles have a "Table of Contents" in the front to help you locate books by page number. Bible apps also have a contents list by book and chapter.

The Bible verses highlighted at the beginning of each lesson in this study are from the New International Version® (NIV®) unless otherwise indicated. You can use any version of the Bible to answer the questions, but using a more easy-to-read translation (NIRV, NLT, NET, ESV) will help you gain confidence in understanding what you are reading. You can find all these translations in the "YouVersion App" or on biblegateway.com.

This study capitalizes certain pronouns referring to God, Jesus and the Holy Spirit—He, Him, His, Himself—just to make the reading of the study information less confusing. Some Bible translations likewise capitalize those pronouns referring to God; others do not. It is simply a matter of preference, not a requirement.

## THE GOD YOU CAN KNOW AND TRUST AS FATHER

*The God You Can Know* lessons focus on the attributes of God—those character qualities of God that He has revealed about Himself. God's greatness is far beyond human understanding. But His Word does give us part of the picture. And that picture reveals an awesome God!

An "attribute" is a quality or characteristic of someone or something. The attributes of God are things we CAN know about God. They describe His character and are true about Him all the time.

God has revealed these attributes about Himself so we can know who He is. By knowing who He is, we can know Him better. He is truly *The God You Can Know*. And by knowing Him, we can learn to trust Him with our lives.

Your God is also a trustworthy Father. Jesus continually taught His disciples to consider God as their Father. This God is your Father God too. The moment you placed your trust in Jesus Christ for your salvation, you were adopted into God's family as His child. He is the perfect Father, the most loving Father, the most dependable Father, and the Father who cares about your every need.

Through these lessons, you will become familiar with the attributes of God that help you to know Him well, love Him wholeheartedly, and gain the confidence to trust Him as your Father God.

## ELEMENTS OF EACH LESSON

This book covers 10 attributes of God in 8 lessons.

1. Each lesson begins with a Bible verse that relates to the focus of the lesson. We recommend that you memorize these verses as they are easy ones for you to learn. The point is to begin the habit of memorizing Scripture. You will be surprised at how soon it just flows from your mind.

2. Start your study with the prayer given after the focus Bible verse. Prayer is just talking to God as conversation with someone who loves you dearly. The beginning prayer simply asks Jesus to teach you through the lesson.

3. This is followed by a simple study of the attribute(s) being covered by the lesson. Read the Bible verses and answer the associated questions. This study uses the NIV translation. We recommend you use that or other easy-to-read translations (CSB, NLT, NET, ESV). See "Bible Basics" above for online sources of these.

4. In the "Trusting Your Father God" section at the end of the study questions, you will be encouraged to dwell more on what you learned in the lesson that applies trusting God as your Father. This will also include times of reflection and prayer.

5. Deeper Discoveries (optional): We have provided additional reading of Bible passages that highlight the attribute of God studied in the lesson. You can spend a few minutes reading and reflecting on what you learn about trusting your Father God from each passage.

## SMALL GROUP DISCUSSION

While you can work through these lessons as a personal study, this study is perfect to use for small groups. Share the following suggested guidelines with the group members to maximize your discussion group experience.

- Set aside some time each week to do the study questions so that you will get to know God better.

- Consistently attend whether your lesson is done or not. You will learn from the discussion.

- Respect each other's insights. Listen thoughtfully. Share your own insights, but do not dominate the discussion.

- Celebrate unity in Christ by avoiding controversial subjects such as politics, divisive issues and denominational differences.

- Maintain confidentiality of whatever is shared within the group.

Enjoy your small group discussion and learn from one another. As you do so, you will have a greater connection with each other. And you'll have more reason to praise our ever-faithful God as you see and hear how He has been faithful to each of you through the years. A small group is a great place to share how you are trusting your Father God in your life.

## Suggested Leader Guide for Group Discussion:

Discussing the lesson (apart from the "Deeper Discoveries" readings) should take about an hour, making this an easy study to fit into a busy workday schedule.

1. Pray for the Lord Jesus to teach you what He wants you to know through the lesson.

2. Work through the LESSON together, reading the Bible verses and discussing the questions. Predetermine which of the explanatory paragraphs you will read as a group. Most simply confirm the truths learned in the questions just asked.

3. Read the "TRUSTING YOUR FATHER GOD" section and share responses to any included application questions.

4. Pray for the group members using the prayer prompts at the end of the lesson.

5. Remind each person to do the next lesson before the group meets again.

# Overview of the Attributes

✓ God's SOVEREIGNTY: God is the sovereign ruler of His creation. He rules it with supreme authority and power.

*"How great you are, O Sovereign LORD! There is no one like you, and there is no God but you, as we have heard with our own ears." (2 Samuel 7:22)*

✓ God's OMNIPOTENCE, OMNIPRESENCE, & OMNISCIENCE *(the Omnis)*: God's power is more powerful than anything or anyone else in the entire universe. God's presence is everywhere at the same time. God knows everything there is to know.

*"You are all around me, behind me and in front of me. You hold me in your power. I'm amazed at how well you know me. It's more than I can understand." (Psalm 139:5-6 NIRV)*

✓ God's HOLINESS: God is holy. He is set apart from anything that is sinful or evil.

*"Your eyes are too pure to look on evil. You cannot tolerate wrongdoing." (Habakkuk 1:13a)*

✓ God's JUSTICE: God always does what is morally right and fair.

*"He did it to demonstrate his righteousness at the present time, so as to be just and the one who justifies those who have faith in Jesus." (Romans 3:26)*

✓ God's GRACE: God's grace is His undeserved favor abundantly poured out on those who desperately need Him.

*"Our Lord poured out more and more of his grace on me. Along with it came faith and love from Christ Jesus." (1 Timothy 1:14 NIRV)*

✓ God's GOODNESS: God is good all the time — even in the tough times, in different ways for each person, and in what He allows or doesn't allow into our lives.

*"You are good, and what you do is good; teach me your decrees." (Psalm 119:68)*

✓ God's LOVE: God's love is patient, kind, forgiving and considers what is best for the one being loved.

*"The Lord is compassionate and gracious, slow to anger, abounding in love." (Psalm 103:8)*

✓ God's JOY: God's joy finds great pleasure in His creation and His creatures, especially people who trust in Him.

*"The joy of the Lord makes you strong." (Nehemiah 8:10 NIRV)*

*Your Father God's love for you is deep and amazing. Bask in it!*

# Enjoy!

# 1: God's Sovereignty

Trusting Your Father God

*"How great you are, O **Sovereign** LORD! There is no one like you, and there is no God but you, as we have heard with our own ears." (2 Samuel 7:22)*

**Pray:** Lord Jesus, please teach me through this lesson.

*The God You Can Know* lessons focus on the attributes of God—those character qualities of God that He has revealed about Himself. God's greatness is far beyond human understanding. But His Word does give us part of the picture. And that picture reveals an awesome God!

An "attribute" is a quality or characteristic of someone or something. For a person, an attribute is something generally true about that person. If someone says that you are always kind, that's an attribute of you. If someone says that you are always generous, that's an attribute of you. Attributes describe someone so that we can know more about him or her.

The attributes of God are things we CAN know about God. They describe His character and are true about Him all the time. God has revealed these attributes about Himself so we can know who He is. By knowing who He is, we can know Him better. He is truly **"the God you can know."** And by knowing Him, we can learn to trust Him with our lives.

Trust (faith) is always an issue of credibility. It is hard to trust God if you don't know Him. The more you know Him, the easier it is to trust Him. You don't have more faith by talking about faith. Getting to know the object of your faith, your God, increases your confidence in Him. Knowing God's character plus His promises gives you plenty of reasons to consider Him trustworthy. The Bible describes that confidence to be like having your feet firmly planted on solid rock—with God as your Rock. He is a trustworthy God.

***What words come to mind when you think about the character of God?***

*Do you feel that He is someone you can know?*

"So I am always thinking that when God reveals a particular thing about Himself, He is helping me know Him. That is the point of saying things about Himself or doing particular things in the world. He is helping me know Him, the true God, a person, so that my delight can be in Him." (John Piper, desiringgod.org, posted on March 8, 2016)

## ATTRIBUTE #1: SOVEREIGNTY

The first attribute we will study is God's SOVEREIGNTY.

*How do you feel about this phrase, "God's sovereignty?"*

*What God says about Himself*

**Read Isaiah 46:9-10.**

*What does God declare about Himself?*

God is sovereign. That is a fact. He is called "Sovereign Lord" over 300 times in the Bible. God is unique among all beings in the entire universe. His counsel, what He determines, will stand without contest. He uses His uniqueness and power to accomplish His own will and purposes without fail. This is God's sovereignty.

The dictionary definition of sovereign is "self-governing, independent, possessing supreme power or authority." At the end of the word "sovereign" is the word "reign." We say that a king "reigns." That means he is the ruler, the one with the right to make the rules. Someone who is sovereign is the ruler, the king, and the one who has the right to make the rules.

*What others recognized about God's sovereignty*

**Read 2 Samuel 7:22 (David).**

*What is declared about God in this verse?*

**Read Deuteronomy 10:14-17 (Moses).**

*What or who is under God's sovereignty (verse 14)?*

*What is true about our sovereign God (verse 17)?*

**Read 1 Samuel 2:6-8 (Hannah).**

*What or who is under God's sovereignty (verse 6)?*

*What or who is under God's sovereignty (verse 7-8)?*

**Read 1 Chronicles 29:11-12 (David).**

*What or who is under God's sovereignty (verse 11)?*

*What or who is under God's sovereignty (verse 12)?*

**Read Psalm 50:10-11 (God speaking through Asaph).**

*What or who is under God's sovereignty?*

**Read Exodus 20:11.**

*About 2 million people heard God speak those words to them. What gives God the right to be king over everything?*

David confirmed what God said about being the one God and no one like Him, His greatness is unequaled. Moses recognized that everything in heaven and earth is His. Hannah recognized that death and life as well as poverty, wealth, and social status are all under God's sovereignty. Asaph wrote the words that God Himself declared about owning every creature of the forest, hills, mountains, and fields.

*As you consider the sovereignty of God from verses you just read, what do you think could stop God's plans from being carried out in your life or in the life of someone you love?*

*Nothing can stop God. He will accomplish anything and everything He has purposed in our lives for our good.*

God Himself told us in many places in the Bible that He created everything. God is sovereign—the king—over the universe, over the earth, over all the creatures on the earth, and over every human being. If you create something, do you have the right to make the rules concerning how your creation should live and work?

We need to think of Him as our sovereign king and be willing to respect Him and obey Him. We can trust His care for His creation, including us. **Our God is the sovereign ruler of His creation who rules it with supreme authority and power.**

## TRUSTING YOUR SOVEREIGN GOD AS A FATHER

If God is the sovereign ruler of His creation, that means He is the sovereign ruler of you. You might bristle at that thought. Yet, your sovereign God is also a trustworthy Father.

**Read Matthew 6:6-9.**

*How are followers of Jesus to think of God (verses 6 and 9)?*

*What does our Father God know (verse 8)?*

**Read Romans 8:14-16.**

*What did the Apostle Paul reveal about our God as a Father?*

**Read 1 John 3:1.**

*What did the Apostle John reveal about our Father God's love for us?*

Jesus continually taught and encouraged His followers to call God, "Father." He taught them to pray to their Father God, whom they could trust. The rest of the New Testament affirms that our Father God's love for His children is deep and amazing.

This God is your Father God too. The moment you placed your trust in Jesus Christ for your salvation, you were adopted into God's family as His child. He is the perfect Father, the most loving Father, the most dependable Father, and the Father who cares about your every need.

Wait a minute. What if you didn't have such a good earthly father! Your concept of a father might be pretty scary. God knows that. But He wants you to know that you are dearly loved by your Father God (Ephesians 5:1; Colossians 3:12).

*Think of the best father in any movie, TV show, or book. Why did that person come to mind?*

God is even better than that father. And through these lessons, you will become familiar with the character of God—those attributes that help you to know Him well, love Him wholeheartedly, and gain the confidence to **trust Him as your Father God**.

Adding together God's sovereignty with His great love expressed through the gift of His Son Jesus should give you security and confidence in Him as your Father God.

Though God is the sovereign ruler of everything, He invites you to come to Him with your needs. You can go to your Father God, ruler over everything, and talk to Him about anything. When you talk to your Father

God, approach Him with humility and respect for His absolute authority. Choose a heart of obedience. He is trustworthy.

*Are you willing to recognize your Father God's authority over you—to trust that He knows what is best for you?*

*If not, why not?*

**Read and reflect on the song lyrics below.**

"You're not a God created by human hands
You're not a God dependent on any mortal man
You're not a God in need of anything we can give
By Your plan, that's just the way it is
You are God alone, from before time began
You were on Your throne, You are God alone.
And right now, in the good times and bad
You are on Your throne, You are God alone.
Unchangeable, unshakable, unstoppable, That's what You are."
(William McDowell, "You Are God Alone" lyrics)

*How does knowing the truths declared about your Father God's sovereignty give you confidence to trust Him today?*

*Pray: Ask your Father God to help you trust in His sovereignty over you.*

## Deeper Discoveries (Optional):

Spend a few minutes reading and reflecting on the following verses that also speak of the sovereignty of God—what the people understood and God's response to their trust in Him.

**Read 2 Kings 19:9-20, 32-36. Jerusalem was being attacked by the king of Assyria. Reflect on what you read.**

**Read Job 38:1-15; 42:1-6. God in His sovereignty had allowed suffering in Job's life for a time. Job questioned why God did this. God's answer to Job and Job's response to God are both consistent with what you have studied in this lesson. Reflect on what you read.**

# 2: God's Power, Presence, & Perception

*"You are **all around me**, behind me and in front of me. You hold me in your **power**. I'm amazed at how well you **know** me. It's more than I can understand." (Psalm 139:5-6 NIRV)*

**Pray:** Lord Jesus, please teach me through this lesson.

## THE GOD YOU CAN KNOW

✓ God's SOVEREIGNTY: God is the sovereign ruler of His creation. He rules it with supreme authority and power.

## ATTRIBUTE #2: THE OMNIS

Remember that an attribute is a word someone could use to describe you that is true all the time. Knowing your attributes will help someone to know you better. Just like that, attributes of our Father God are those descriptions of God that tell us who He is so that we can know Him better, and by knowing Him better, we can trust Him as our Father. We have a God we can know.

Lesson 1 covered God's Sovereignty. In this lesson, we will be studying three of God's attributes sometimes called "the Omnis." The word *omni* means "all." The attributes of God that are the Omnis are: 1) omnipotence, 2) omnipresence, and 3) omniscience. Let's break them down and see what they mean.

## OMNIPOTENCE

God's OMNIPOTENCE. We know the first part "omni" means all and the second part "potence" means powerful. So putting those two together, we get "all powerful." Omnipotence refers to God's power. God is all powerful—more powerful than anything or anyone else in the entire universe.

*Name some things or some people you think are powerful. After each one, say, "God is more powerful than that."*

## What God says about Himself

**Read Genesis 1:3, 6, 9.**

*What did God declare and what happened?*

Nowhere is God's omnipotence seen more clearly than in creation. God said, "Let there be…" and it was so. Humans need tools and materials to create. God simply spoke, and by the power of His word, everything was created from nothing. That's one big demonstration and evidence of His omnipotence.

**Read Matthew 19:23-26.**

*What did Jesus, as God the Son, declare about the power of God?*

The Lord had said basically the same thing to Sarah and Abraham in Genesis 18:14. Nothing is too hard for the Lord.

## What others say about God's omnipotence

You won't read the word "omnipotence" in the Bible, but you will read many words that describe God's power. One particular name of God refers to His omnipotence. That name is "Almighty." God is called "the Almighty" or "Lord Almighty" 345 times in the Bible. The prophet Jeremiah in the Old Testament talked about God's power a lot and called Him the Lord Almighty.

**Read Jeremiah 32:17.**

*What did God use His power to do?*

*What did Jeremiah say was too hard for God?*

*When you think of God's power, what comes to your mind?*

God uses His power to do many things—to create and to perform miracles like parting the Red Sea, winning battles, and healing people. Every time Jesus healed someone, that was God's power at work. Anyone who trusts in God can experience His power.

**Read Ephesians 1:19-20.**

*What did Paul pray for you as a believer to know (verse 19)?*

*What did God's power do (verse 20)?*

*For whom is God's power at work (verse 19)?*

God's power raised Jesus, who had died on the cross—raised Him up alive and with a new body that would never die again. That's pretty powerful, isn't it?

**Read Ephesians 3:20.**

*Our powerful God is able to do what?*

*God's power is at work where?*

*God uses His power to work for us and in us. And we can ask Him to do that in our lives.*

That's the first omni — omnipotence, which means all powerful. **God is more powerful than anything or anyone else in the entire universe.**

## OMNIPRESENCE

The second omni is OMNIPRESENCE, which means "all presence." When we say that God has "all presence" we mean that God is present everywhere at the same time. There isn't any place in the entire universe where God cannot be found. God is present everywhere at the same time.

*What God says about Himself*

**Read Jeremiah 23:23-24.**

*What did God declare about His presence?*

**Read Matthew 18:20.**

*What did Jesus as God declare about His presence?*

## *What others recognized about God's omnipresence*

The truth of God being present everywhere is so well described in Psalm 139. The psalms are songs written by those who loved God and wanted to speak or sing His praises.

**Read Psalm 139:5.**

*David was talking to God as he wrote. How did he describe God's presence with him?*

**Read Psalm 139:7-10.**

*Where can you go to get away from God?*

*Is there any place far enough away that He can't find you? Or can someone hide you so God can't find you?*

*Can you go to a place where God is not with you or cannot hear you calling out to Him?*

The Bible teaches that God is everywhere at the same time. God is near you as you go about your daily schedule—to work, school, stores, or home. God is near you at each place. God is with you everywhere. In fact, wherever you go…He is already there! Even in the worst situation or location, you might not get a cell signal, but God is not blocked out! Ever!

**How does that give you comfort?**

**When are some times that you need to remember that God is always wherever you are?**

David, in his psalm, reminded himself that God was not only there but that His hand would be holding him close (verse 10). And he declared that God is still there with him even while he is sleeping.

*Next time you are scared or hurt or in life's dark places, remember that God is with you right then. Picture Him holding your hand and gain comfort from that.*

So the second omni is omnipresence, which means all presence. **God is present everywhere at the same time.**

## OMNISCIENCE

The third omni is OMNISCIENCE. It's spelled *omni-science*. So it does mean God knows everything there is to know about science. But it's more than that. Our word "science" comes from an old Latin word that means "to know" or "knowing." So when we talk about God's omniscience, we are saying that God is "all knowing." That means that God knows everything there is to know. [Note: the word "perception" in the lesson title means "to know."]

*What God says about Himself*

**Read Matthew 6:8, 31-32.**

*What does your Father God know?*

**Read Matthew 9:3-4 and Luke 6:7-8.**

*What does Jesus as God's Son know?*

God knows your needs before you even tell Him about them. God knows your thoughts so He is not surprised by what you think or say.

*What others recognized about God's omniscience*

God's omniscience can really baffle our minds. But let's talk about how that affects us personally. David wrote about this in Psalm 139.

**Read Psalm 139:1-4.**

*Write Psalm 139:1 in the space below.*

*What does God know about you (verse 2)?*

*What does God know about you (verse 3)?*

*What does God know about you (verse 4)?*

*Can you hide anything from God? Does anything good or bad in your life escape His notice or surprise Him?*

Read Psalm 139:13-14.

*What does know about you?*

*Knowing that God knows you well—having created you to be the special, unique person you are—how does your heart feel about that?*

*God knows what is going on in your life. He also knows what is going on deep in your heart. And He knows what is best for you!*

The third omni is omniscience, which means, "all knowing." **God knows everything there is to know** about everything.

The *Omnis* are three truths that are characteristics of God alone. Putting those truths together would be saying that **God is more powerful than anything or anyone else in the entire universe, is present everywhere at the same time, and knows everything there is to know.**

## TRUSTING YOUR FATHER GOD'S POWER, PRESENCE, AND PERCEPTION

So how does knowing about God's omnipotence, omnipresence, and omniscience affect your life? The truth you need to know and remember from this lesson is this: **God is always near you, He knows what is going on in your life, and He can do something about it.**

*How should knowing this truth give you confidence in Him to handle anything?*

Think of those 3 Omnis as a chair. When you sit on a chair, you get to rest. Your Father God wants you to rest knowing that He is always near you, He knows what is going on in your life, and He can do something about it. The Bible says that you can rest on that.

Knowing about God is a good thing. But more important is being known by God. Your Father God knows you and loves you. Trust is the proper response to the God who knows your needs, your wants, your thoughts, and your heart.

When you talk to your Father God, humbly realize He can do anything. And although He cares about every detail in your life, think about how small your problems are compared with how awesome your Father God is! Tell God about your deepest concern then wait and see what your Father God does. You can trust Him in whatever He chooses to do for any situation you find yourself in today, tomorrow or the next day.

*What is your deepest concern right now? Can you trust Him in whatever He chooses to do for that situation?*

Pray: Ask your Father God to help you trust that He is always near you, that He knows what is going on in your life, and that He can do something about it.

Spend a few minutes reading and reflecting on the following verses that also speak of the "omnis" of God.

**Read all of Psalm 139. Reflect on all that God knows about you and how that should affect your value of yourself.**

**Read 2 Chronicles 20:1-30. Reflect on what you read— what the people understood and God's response to their trust in Him.**

# 3: God's Holiness

*"Your eyes are too pure to look on evil. You
cannot tolerate wrongdoing..." (Habakkuk 1:13)*

---

**Pray:** *Lord Jesus, please teach me through this lesson.*

---

## THE GOD YOU CAN KNOW

✓ God's SOVEREIGNTY: God is the sovereign ruler of His creation.
  He rules it with supreme authority and power.

✓ God's OMNIPOTENCE, OMNIPRESENCE, & OMNISCIENCE (the
  Omnis): God's power is more powerful than anything or anyone else
  in the entire universe. God's presence is everywhere at the same
  time. God knows everything there is to know.

## ATTRIBUTE #3: HOLINESS

This lesson is about God's HOLINESS.

***When you read the word "holiness," what comes to your
mind?***

Holiness is the state or quality of being holy. "Holy" is used more than
any other word in the Bible to describe God so it must be very important.
God is called "the Holy One of Israel" and "the Holy God." The word
"holy" by itself means, "to set apart." That means one thing is totally
separated from something else. Holiness thus means "to be set apart."
So our holy God is totally set apart from something. The question to ask
is, "From what?"

*What God says about Himself*

**Read Leviticus 11:44-45.**

**What does God declare about Himself?**

The Bible teaches that our God is set apart from these:

- *Set apart from any other name.* God's name is holy. His name is set apart from any other name in the entire universe. That includes the names of other gods that people want to worship instead of the one true God.

- *Set apart from His creation.* God is not like anything or anyone He has created. That includes angels and people. God is set apart from His creation.

- *Set apart from anything that is sinful or evil.* In fact, this is what is stressed the most about God in the Bible. He is the most "holy," and no one is as "holy" as He is. He is perfect.

  "The word holy calls attention to all that God is. It reminds us that His love is holy love, His justice is holy justice, His mercy is holy mercy, His knowledge is holy knowledge, His spirit is holy spirit." (R. C. Sproul, The Holiness of God, p. 57)

*What others recognized about God's holiness*

**Read Habakkuk 1:13.**

Habakkuk lived at the time of the Babylonian invasion of Jerusalem (~600 BC).

**How did Habakkuk describe God at the beginning of the verse?**

In God's holiness, He cannot even look on evil or wrongdoing. It is a unique part of His character—who He is. God's holiness sets Him apart from anything that is sinful or evil.

*If God is perfectly good all the time, what are some things that God cannot do?*

**Read James 1:13.**

*What is something else that God will not do?*

*It is very comforting to know that our God can be trusted to be good all the time. Can human beings be perfectly good all the time?*

*Evil and wrongdoing that people do are called "sin" in the Bible. Give some examples of human sins.*

When God created humans, He designed them to have a relationship with Him. Because Adam and Eve disobeyed God, sin entered the world. You can read about this in Genesis chapter 3. Adam and Eve became separated from the perfect fellowship they had with God. And all people born after them were born sinners. What a bummer!

But if humans are sinful, this creates a problem because God is set apart from sin. That's His holiness. He hates sin and must judge it. The Bible tells us that our sins separate us from Him. But God doesn't want us to be separated from Him forever. So He made a way to bring us back to Him. Yet, this meant getting rid of our sin.

God had a marvelous plan. His own Son would come to earth to be born as a baby, grow up to live as a human just like us, and die for our sins so we could be forgiven of them. That's the wonder of Christmas. At Christmas, we celebrate God's absolutely marvelous plan. When we trust in Jesus, He will remove our sin from us so we are no longer separated from Him. What an amazing gift!

**Read Isaiah 1:18.**

*What is God's promise to you?*

During your school days, did you have a teacher who marked wrong answers with red ink? Red usually says, "That's wrong. That's not acceptable." When God says our sins are bright red, He is saying the wrong things we do are not acceptable to a holy God.

*What do you think the phrase "white as snow" means?*

Freshly fallen snow looks so pristine, doesn't it? Pure and clean. The phrase "white like wool" refers to freshly prepared sheep's wool that is perfectly clean and hasn't been dyed with any colors yet. It's also pure and clean. That's what God does to our sin the moment we trust in Jesus so we can get close to Him as our Father God.

And here is the absolutely even-more-wonderful part: as we live each day as believers in Jesus, God continues to cleanse our sin from us so we can be close to Him.

*We can enjoy our relationship with a holy God who loves us dearly, the kind of relationship that He created us to enjoy.*

**Read 2 Corinthians 5:21.**

*What does God do to your sin?*

*What do you get from Christ?*

When God looks at us, He doesn't see sin in our lives. Jesus takes away our sin. We are no longer separated from our holy God. He sees Jesus' righteousness instead. Our sins are washed white as snow. This is called, "The Great Exchange." Jesus takes our sin; we receive His righteousness. We can only marvel at God's goodness to us in this gift.

**Read 1 Peter 1:14-16.**

*What does God desire for you (verses 14-15)?*

*Why (verses 15-16)?*

Holiness means "to be set apart." God desires that we would choose to live set apart from anything that is sinful or evil. Then, we would reflect His character in our own lives.

**Read 1 Corinthians 10:13.**

*What does God promise to you when you are tempted to sin?*

*What confidence does knowing this give you?*

Temptation to do wrong is part of life here on earth. Those temptations are not coming from God. Instead, He provides a way of escape for every temptation so that you can stand firm against it. That's His promise.

**God's holiness means He is set apart from anything that is sinful or evil.**

## Reflecting God's holiness

We are created in God's image, and we can share in many of His attributes in our daily lives like love, mercy, and faithfulness. But some of God's attributes, such as omnipresence, omniscience, and omnipotence, will never be shared by created beings. Holiness is also like that. As we continue to live in our earthly bodies, we will not be completely holy as God is holy. We only become holy by faith in Jesus Christ as God. God cleanses us from sin when we trust in Jesus so that we are no longer separated from Him. God declares us holy in His sight (Colossians 1:22). Through His Spirit inside us He also helps us live as holy people, set apart from sin in our own lives.

**Read 1 Chronicles 16:28-29 and Psalm 99:9.**

*What is the proper response to God's holiness?*

**Read 1 Peter 1:14-19.**

*What is the proper response to God's holiness?*

## TRUSTING YOUR FATHER GOD'S HOLINESS

Your Father God is a holy God. That means He will never lie to you, cheat you, or desert you. He is trustworthy because of His holiness.

As you approach your Father God, you can thank Him for His marvelous plan and for continuing to cleanse you of sin so you aren't separated from Him ever again. You can trust Him to always be good to you and those you love.

Reverence your Father God in your heart as the Holy One. Grasping His holiness will lead you to desire to be like Him in hating and avoiding evil. You can trust Him to never tempt you to do anything wrong.

**Read the familiar hymn below.**

> "Holy, holy, holy! Lord God Almighty
> Early in the morning our song shall rise to Thee
> Holy, holy, holy! Merciful and mighty
> God in three persons Blessed Trinity!
> Holy, holy, holy! Though the darkness hide thee
> Though the eye of sinful man Thy glory may not see
> Only Thou art holy There is none beside Thee
> Perfect in power, in love and purity"
> ("Holy, Holy, Holy Lord God Almighty," lyrics by 18th century
> Anglican bishop Reginald Heber)

*What response does God's holiness inspire in you?*

---

*Pray: Ask your Father God to help you appreciate His holiness and lead you to desire to be like Him in hating and avoiding evil.*

## DEEPER DISCOVERIES (OPTIONAL):

Spend a few minutes reading and reflecting on the following verses that also speak of the "holiness" of God and why you can trust Him.

**Read Romans 8:1-11, 28-39. Reflect on all that your holy God does for you and how you should respond to Him for that.**

**Read Isaiah 6:1-10. Reflect on what you learn about God's holiness and your proper response.**

# 4: God's Justice

*"He did it to demonstrate his righteousness at the present time, so as to be **just** and the one who justifies those who have faith in Jesus." (Romans 3:26)*

## THE GOD YOU CAN KNOW

- ✓ God's SOVEREIGNTY: God is the sovereign ruler of His creation. He rules it with supreme authority and power.

- ✓ God's OMNIPOTENCE, OMNIPRESENCE, & OMNISCIENCE (the Omnis): God's power is more powerful than anything or anyone else in the entire universe. God's presence is everywhere at the same time. God knows everything there is to know.

- ✓ God's HOLINESS: God is holy. He is set apart from anything that is sinful or evil.

## ATTRIBUTE #4: JUSTICE

God's holiness is related to another attribute which we will study in this lesson—God's JUSTICE.

### When are you likely to want justice?




The concept of justice means that someone should be concerned with two things—being right and being fair. Justice means, "always doing what is morally right and fair." That's how you likely want to be treated by others whenever there is a problem, isn't it? You want them to do what is right and to be fair about it.

Our God always acts with justice. It is the natural expression of His holiness. Remember we said that God's holiness always sets Him apart from anything that is sinful or evil. The Bible says that God hates sin and has declared that sin is wrong and must be punished by death.

## What God says about Himself

**Read Isaiah 61:8.**

*What did God declare about Himself?*

## What others recognized about God's justice

**Read Deuteronomy 32:3-4.**

*What did Moses declare about God's justice?*

**Read Psalm 119:137-138.**

*What did the psalmist declare about God's justice?*

Because God is a holy God and all His ways are just, He can never accept sin. His response to sin is to declare it wrong and demand punishment for it. That is justice, even as we humans understand it.

The Apostle Paul wrote about God's justice in the book of Romans.

**Read Romans 1:18-20.**

*Why is God just in His dealings with humans?*

**Read Romans 3:23.**

*What does this verse declare about all people, including you?*


**Read Romans 5:12.**

*What happened to all people, including you, because of sin?*


Since everyone has sinned, everyone is declared guilty of sin by God's justice. He's being right and fair. And each guilty person must pay a penalty. The Bible says the penalty for sin is death. That's God's justice. **God's justice always does what is morally right and fair.** It's fair for God to say anyone who sins must be declared guilty and pay a penalty.

In our society, whenever a person is declared guilty of committing a crime, they have to pay the penalty for what they did wrong. They usually go to prison and are held captive in prison until the penalty is paid—maybe 3 months or 2 years, sometimes 20 years or more.

In the Old Testament, God decided that certain animals would die to pay the penalty for the sins of people. By the deaths of those animals, called "sacrifices," the people would be set free from being guilty for a little while, until the people did bad things again. But this was only a temporary plan.

God had a better plan. He loves people so much that He came to earth Himself as a man named Jesus who lived a perfect life and died on the cross as the sacrifice for our sins. Jesus paid the penalty for sin that God's justice demands. Jesus paid this penalty for us so that we would not have to do it nor would any animals ever have to do it again!

Paul described it beautifully in Romans 3.

**Read Romans 3:24-26.**

*How is God's justice satisfied (verse 25)?*

*Why did God do this (verse 26)?*

God's justice is right and fair. The NIRV translation of verse 26 clearly describes this:

> *"God did that to prove in our own time that he is **fair**. He proved that he is **right**. He also made **right** with himself those who believe in Jesus." (Romans 3:26 NIRV)*

God demonstrates for us what it means to be morally right and fair. And He desires that we live life His way, according to His character.

**Read Micah 6:8.**

**What does God ask of you to live life according to His ways?**

**God's justice always does what is morally right and fair.** He desires that we uphold justice in our lives as well. The New Testament writings teach us how to live life God's way, following the example of Jesus Christ. God will enable you to live that way. He wants you to live that way. Is that something you'd like to do?

## TRUSTING YOUR FATHER GOD'S JUSTICE

Jesus paid the penalty for every wrong thing that anyone has ever done or will do in the future. God's justice is satisfied. So God can declare that anyone who trusts in Jesus is "set free" from having to pay the penalty for their sin. Everyone who trusts in Jesus is free from being held captive by his or her sins.

What a great deal! Being set free is a great thing. God's justice sets free everyone who trusts that His Son Jesus Christ paid the penalty for their sins. God can do that because the penalty has been paid for all time.

When you trust in Jesus you receive complete forgiveness for ALL of your sins. This sets you free from being afraid of God.

*Isn't it easier to not be afraid of God if you know that He forgives you for all the bad things you do? Instead, you can be confident that God loves you dearly.*

**Have you lived in fear of God, being afraid of Him?**

**How does the truth that you are set free from being afraid of God make you feel now?**

And if you aren't afraid of God, you are set free to love Him back with your whole heart. Isn't that true? It's easier to love someone that you know loves you!

**Have you learned to love your Father God? How do you express your love for Him?**

Pray: Ask your Father God to help you appreciate His justice and to show you how to do for others what is morally right and fair just like He does for you.

Spend a few minutes reading and reflecting on the following verses that also speak of the "justice" of God and why you can trust Him.

**Read Romans 3:10-26. Reflect on what God in His justice has done for you.**

**Read Psalm 89:1-15. Reflect on how a believer should respond when knowing God's character.**

# 5: God's Grace

*"Our Lord poured out more and more of his* **grace** *on me. Along with it came faith and love from Christ Jesus." (1 Timothy 1:14 NIRV)*

**Pray:** Lord Jesus, please teach me through this lesson.

## THE GOD YOU CAN KNOW

- ✓ God's SOVEREIGNTY: God is the sovereign ruler of His creation. He rules it with supreme authority and power.
- ✓ God's OMNIPOTENCE, OMNIPRESENCE, & OMNISCIENCE (the Omnis): God's power is more powerful than anything or anyone else in the entire universe. God's presence is everywhere at the same time. God knows everything there is to know.
- ✓ God's HOLINESS: God is holy. He is set apart from anything that is sinful or evil.
- ✓ God's JUSTICE: God always does what is morally right and fair.

## ATTRIBUTE #5: GRACE

Now, we are going to learn about God's GRACE.

**What do you think "grace" means?**

You may know some girls or women named Grace or Gracie. A lot of churches have the word "grace" as part of their name. One of the most well-known songs worldwide is "Amazing Grace."

For Christians, "grace" is a very special word. You've probably heard the word but may not know what it means. Grace means "undeserved favor." **God's grace is His undeserved favor abundantly poured out on those who desperately need Him.**

*What God says about Himself*

**Read Exodus 34:5-6.**

*What does God declare about Himself?*

*What others recognized about God's grace*

**Read Psalm 103:8-12.**

*What is said about God in verse 8?*

*In His graciousness, what does He not do (verses 9-10)?*

*In His graciousness, what does He do for us (verse 12)?*

I mentioned the song "Amazing Grace" earlier in this lesson. That song was written by a man named John Newton who lived 300 years ago and understood the immensity of God's grace in his life.

When John was a boy, his mother taught him Bible stories and prayed that he would grow up to become a minister. Sadly, when he was only 6, his mother died. His father was a ship captain who would be gone for months or years at a time. His new stepmother didn't want him and ignored him. So John was lonely and angry, rebelling against everything his mother taught him.

One night, John was kidnapped and dragged onto an English war ship to work as a sailor. Even angrier, he refused to follow the captain's orders and was often whipped and put in chains. His rotten attitude and language were worse than that of the other sailors. And John made fun of anyone who believed in God. He thought that life had treated him badly, so John decided to be cruel to others. John Newton got his own ship and became a slave trader. He chained African people in his ship, and sailed them to North America to be sold as slaves. The bad boy became a bad man.

One day, a violent storm began to rip his ship apart. John felt helpless and very afraid because he couldn't swim. Suddenly, he remembered Bible verses his mother had taught him. John cried out to God, "Lord, have mercy on us!" But then he thought, "What mercy can there be for a *wretch* like me?" A wretch is a wicked, unhappy person. John told God he was sorry for turning away from Him and for doing so much wrong. The storm ended, and John's life was spared. He knew that God had done that for him!

Then, John found a Bible and read how Jesus could forgive him for all the bad things he had done. John Newton trusted in Jesus to forgive him. Over time, he stopped cussing, being angry all the time, and being a slave trader. In fact, he joined others who fought against the slave trade in England. Before he died, it was outlawed.

His mother had prayed for him to become a minister. God answered that prayer with a "Yes." John became the pastor of several churches, traveled around England telling how God saved a wretch like him.

As stated at the beginning of this lesson, the word "grace" means "undeserved favor." In the Bible, grace is God giving favor to someone, not because they are good enough to deserve it but because His love chooses to do so.

Did John Newton deserve God's favor? No. He even called himself a wretch—a wicked, unhappy person. Yet, when he trusted Jesus, God's grace saved John from death, completely forgave him for all his sins, and gave him a brand-new life.

## *What Jesus revealed about God's grace*

John Newton's story is much like the prodigal son in the Bible. Jesus told the story of a family with 2 sons. The younger son told his dad one day that he wanted to take his share of the family money and go away to see the world rather than stay home and help his dad run the farm. So he did. But he was very reckless with his money and spent it all while doing bad things—like John Newton did when he was away from home.

Desperate, this younger son got a job feeding pigs. But even that wasn't enough for him to buy enough food for himself. He was miserable. So he decided to go back home and ask his dad to let him be a servant. What do you think his father did? Was he angry with him for leaving in the first place and spending all his money? Or was he happy to see his young son again? Let's find out.

**Read Luke 15:11-24.**

*Focusing on verse 20, what was the father doing?*

*What actions did he take when he saw his boy coming home?*

*Did his dad have a little bit of love for his boy or a lot of love?*

*Why did the father celebrate (verses 24 and 32)?*

The prodigal son didn't deserve his father's favor. But his dad was looking for him to come home. That is a picture of God's abundant grace as taught throughout the Bible.

**Read 1 Timothy 1:13-15.**

*How did Paul describe himself (verses 13 and 15)?*

*How did Paul describe God's grace (verse 14)?*

*What image comes to mind when you think of something being poured out abundantly?*

Paul was describing himself in his letter. But doesn't it also describe John Newton and what God did for him? No longer was John the bad man, the slave trader, but became John, the beloved child of God, the one who taught many people about Jesus. John Newton wrote "Amazing Grace," the song that has become one of the favorite songs of all time. When John Newton was writing the song, he remembered that terrible storm and how wonderful it was to be right with God at last. He praised God for His grace. This is what he wrote:

> "Amazing grace! How sweet the sound that saved a wretch like me! I once was lost, but now am found; was blind, but now I see. 'Twas grace that taught my heart to fear, and grace my fears relieved; How precious did that grace appear the hour I first believed! Through many dangers, toils and snares, I have already come; 'Tis grace hath brought me safe thus far, and grace will lead me home." (John Newton, 18th century pastor)

*When he wrote "the hour I first believed," when was that?*

**God's grace is His undeserved favor abundantly poured out on those who desperately need him.** His grace overflows to you every single day. You are completely forgiven and covered in God's grace.

*God gives His favor to someone not because they are good enough to deserve it but because **His love chooses to do so**. We all receive it when we trust in Jesus. Isn't God's grace amazing!*

## TRUSTING YOUR FATHER GOD'S GRACE

Remember how that prodigal son's father was so filled with love he was ready to forgive his son for all the bad things he did and welcome him home? That's how Father God welcomed John Newton home to Him. That's how your Father God welcomed you when you trusted in Jesus.

*Have you ever thought you were too sinful for God to save? Why did you think that?*

If you thought that, then grace is the good news God has for you. Your salvation is not based upon how good you are or any works you do. It is entirely based on your faith in Jesus Christ. In Him, you are completely forgiven and welcomed into the arms of your Father God. The Apostle Paul called himself the "chief of sinners" (1 Timothy 1:15). You would have to stand in line behind Paul and John Newton if you wish to think of yourself as too sinful.

*Reread 1 Timothy 1:13-14. Make these verses personal. Replace Paul's experience with your own experience.*

God's absolutely amazing grace comes to you in abundance the moment you trust in Christ. You are accepted, forgiven, declared holy, and dearly loved from that moment onward.

Yes, you may have to live with the consequences of your sinfulness. But God's grace will give you the strength and help to get through that as well.

*Use any creative means to express gratitude for God's amazing grace toward you—drawing, painting, prose, poetry, song, or prayer. This is your prayer and praise to God today.*

## DEEPER DISCOVERIES (OPTIONAL):

Spend a few minutes reading and reflecting on the following verses that also speak of the "grace" of God and why you can trust Him.

**Read Psalm 103. Reflect on the writer's understanding of the grace of God.**

**Read John 8:2-11. Reflect on how Jesus demonstrated God's grace toward the woman.**

# 6: God's Goodness

*"You [God] are **good**, and what you do is **good**; teach me your decrees." (Psalm 119:68)*

**Pray:** Lord Jesus, please teach me through this lesson.

## THE GOD YOU CAN KNOW

- ✓ God's SOVEREIGNTY: God is the sovereign ruler of His creation. He rules it with supreme authority and power.
- ✓ God's OMNIPOTENCE, OMNIPRESENCE, & OMNISCIENCE (the Omnis): God's power is more powerful than anything or anyone else in the entire universe. God's presence is everywhere at the same time. God knows everything there is to know.
- ✓ God's HOLINESS: God is holy. He is set apart from anything that is sinful or evil.
- ✓ God's JUSTICE: God always does what is morally right and fair.
- ✓ God's GRACE: God's grace is His undeserved favor abundantly poured out on those who desperately need Him.

## ATTRIBUTE #6: GOODNESS

Our lesson today will focus on God's GOODNESS.

**When we say that someone is a good person, what are we usually talking about?**

You might think of someone who never does anything wrong, who always does everything right. You might think of someone who is very kind and generous. Well, God is the ultimate one who is good, who "always does everything right and is always kind and generous." Let's talk about what that really means.

## What God says about Himself

The goodness of God is prominent in the first chapters of the Bible. God pronounced all that He had made to be "good." But when He recognized something that was not good (Adam being alone in Genesis 2), God took care of that by creating a wife for him.

**Read Exodus 33:19.**

**What does God declare about Himself?**

Our Lord Jesus is also good. This is usually represented in how He is portrayed in movies and paintings.

**Why do you think artists or movies almost always present Jesus wearing white clothes?**

Though Jesus is presented as wearing white, He probably didn't wear white. Men back then wore clothes that were dyed with colors or left a natural looking tan. And remember they didn't have washing machines so no one's clothes would have stayed white for very long!

Using white clothes helps the audience to identify Jesus because we don't have any photos to know what He looked like. You always know the man in white is Jesus. Perhaps your answer to the above question was that white represents Jesus as being perfect because He never did any of the bad things called sin. That's a reasonable answer. White would definitely represent His purity.

That white color also represents His goodness. One time when Jesus was on a mountain with Peter, James and John, something happened to His clothes.

**Read Mark 9:2-8.**

*On the mountain, how did His appearance change (verse 3)?*

*What did God the Father say about Him (verse 7)?*

Jesus' clothes became dazzling white, whiter than anyone in the world could ever bleach them. This was to show His disciples that He really was God. Jesus is the God-man who never sinned. The color white represents His goodness. And God is good all the time.

That's an important truth for you to know and trust. "**GOD IS GOOD ALL THE TIME**."

*What others recognized about God's goodness*

**Read Psalm 119:68.**

*What does this verse (addressed to God) say about God?*

**Read Psalm 145:9.**

*What did the writer declare about God?*

**Read James 1:17.**

*What did James (the half-brother of Jesus) declare about God?*

The Bible says that everything about God is good—He is good in Himself and what He does is good. That means God allows nothing to happen to His children—to those who love Him—that is not for their good. God gives to His children only that which is good. **God is good all the time**, and He is at work in our lives for good.

**Read Romans 8:28.**

*What is promised about God at work in our lives?*




But you might ask, what about the tough things that happen to us? Someone gets very sick, loses a job, or has to move far away from family and friends. Is God being good then? What must be the answer to that question? YES! Why? Because **God is good all the time**.

Over the years, I've learned through personal Bible study and my faith walk that God's goodness has three aspects that apply to our times of fear and pain: 1) He is good even in the tough times; 2) He is good in different ways to each of us; and 3) He is good in what He allows or doesn't allow into our lives. Let's consider each of those.

*Truth #1: God is good even in the tough times.*

As a child, did your parents or other authority ever make you do something that was hard to do? As an adult, have you ever tasked children or students with things that were hard to do, perhaps very hard, in order for them to learn a new skill? No doubt the answer to both questions is, "Yes, of course!"

God is the perfect parent and knows what will help His children grow into maturity. That sometimes includes pain. Isn't that true regarding human parents and children? Growing up is hard just in the facing of new things while getting used to the old. Teething hurts, but babies must go through teething to get some teeth to chew real food. The same thing is true of learning to walk or ride a bike. And what about adolescence? That is a long, painful, but necessary time of gaining independence. Coddling of children prevents them from growing up.

God teaches His children through tough things that He allows in our lives that help us grow up. Those tough things build bones and teeth in our faith. They help us learn to trust God. They help us learn to give up trying to do things our own way—which may not be the best way—and start doing things God's way—which is always the best way. **Anything** that draws us closer to God is good for us!

The Bible tells about 2 women named Naomi and Ruth who experienced some very tough times. Naomi is an older woman who had left her home in Bethlehem to travel with her husband and their two sons to a neighboring country called Moab. They did this to find food. The sons married girls from Moab. One of those girls was named Ruth. But some bad things happened to the family.

### Read Ruth 1:1-22.

*What hurtful things did Naomi experience?*

*What hurtful things did Ruth experience?*

Naomi's husband died. Then, Naomi's sons died. That means Ruth's husband died. Both women were left alone. Naomi was very sad and decided to go back home to Bethlehem. Ruth joined her. They had to trust God to provide food for the journey and in the town. That brought them both closer to God. Ruth spent a day gleaning in the fields of a kind relative so that she and Naomi had plenty to eat that night.

### Read Ruth 2:17-20.

*What did Naomi declare about God in verse 20 in spite of all that she had experienced?*

God had not stopped showing His kindness even in the tough times because **God is good all the time.** So truth #1 is this: God is good even in the tough times.

## Truth #2: God is good in different ways for each person.

God's goodness may look different in my life than it does in your life. Have you or someone in your family been very sick? Or have you moved away from home to a place far away? When that happened, you may have felt sad, scared, or lonely. It's hard to move, especially from a familiar place to a new place. Yet, because of moving, God's goodness often gives you a new friend who is so happy to have you living near her. God was good to that person in a different way by moving you and providing a new friend.

Sometimes you can't feel it or see it. Something that looks bad for one person may be just what that person needs to get to know God in a very personal way. Or it may be just what another person who is watching needs in order to know God in a personal way.

In the Bible story about Naomi and Ruth, Naomi and her family found food in Moab when they needed it. That was good. But Ruth didn't need food. She needed God. Her people in Moab didn't know God. So God sent Naomi to be a missionary to Ruth in Moab, to tell her about the true God so Ruth could believe in Him. God was being good to Ruth and Naomi in different ways. Truth #2 is this: God is good in different ways for each person.

> **Are you willing to recognize that God is good to you in a way that is different from how He is good to others?**

## Truth #3: God is good in what He allows or doesn't allow into our lives

In the story about Naomi and Ruth, Naomi's sons both died as young men, but that doesn't happen to everyone. Not everyone gets sick with cancer or has a car accident. Not every person moves far away from home. Throughout the Bible are many verses stating how God healed someone or protected someone in a dangerous situation. We don't even know all the dangers God is protecting us from daily! We should thank

Him all the time for doing that. Truth #3 is this: God blocks out more hard things in our lives than He allows to happen to us.

*Are you ready to trust that what He does allow into your life is for your good?*

*God is good all the time—even in the tough times, in different ways for each person, and in what He allows or doesn't allow into our lives.*

God works good. God is God!

## TRUSTING YOUR FATHER GOD'S GOODNESS

As we learned in Lesson 1, Jesus presented God as a good Father. He knows your needs and knows how best to meet your needs.

As I mentioned above, trusting His choice of how to meet that need is the sticky part. Why is that? It is often because you and I may already have an idea of what we think His goodness to us should look like! We are all good at praying solutions to whatever is challenging us. "Here's the need, God. Here's how you can fix it. Wouldn't that be a good idea, God?"

And waiting is hard. Do you realize that whenever you are waiting for a situation to be resolved, God is waiting right along with you? We must wait for God's "always perfect" timing in answer to our prayers.

*Is this a problem for you? Have you become discouraged (or been discouraged in the past) from having to wait?*

Do you and I really believe that God has the right to choose what He brings into our lives, including having to wait for it? I know God is good. And anything that makes us depend on Him more is good for us. So it is your choice to trust His choice of how to be good to you. Count on God's goodness and trust His choosing!

"Sometimes the reality of God's goodness doesn't perfectly fit into our idea of goodness, and that's okay. In fact, it's fantastic because the goodness that God has in store for His children is infinitely more wonderful than anything we could conceive on our own." (Reagan Rodgers, "Silver Linings")

*As you talk to your Father God, are you willing to trust His goodness in the way He chooses to answer your prayer?*

*Pray: Ask God to help you believe that He is good all the time even in the tough times in life. Thank God for the many tough things He doesn't allow into your life.*

## DEEPER DISCOVERIES (OPTIONAL):

Spend a few minutes reading and reflecting on the following verses that also speak of the "goodness" of God and why you can trust Him.

Read Psalm 73. Reflect on what the writer realizes after he complains about all the unfairness he sees in the world.

Read Psalm 107. Reflect on the ways God was good to those in different situations of life.

# 7: God's Love

*"The Lord is compassionate and gracious, slow to anger, abounding in **love**." (Psalm 103:8)*

> **Pray:** Lord Jesus, please teach me through this lesson.

## THE GOD YOU CAN KNOW

✓ God's SOVEREIGNTY: God is the sovereign ruler of His creation. He rules it with supreme authority and power.

✓ God's OMNIPOTENCE, OMNIPRESENCE, & OMNISCIENCE (the Omnis): God's power is more powerful than anything or anyone else in the entire universe. God's presence is everywhere at the same time. God knows everything there is to know.

✓ God's HOLINESS: God is holy. He is set apart from anything that is sinful or evil.

✓ God's JUSTICE: God always does what is morally right and fair.

✓ God's GRACE: God's grace is His undeserved favor abundantly poured out on those who desperately need Him.

✓ God's GOODNESS: God is good all the time — even in the tough times, in different ways for each person, and in what He allows or doesn't allow into our lives.

## ATTRIBUTE #7: LOVE

Today, our lesson is about God's LOVE—**for** you and loving others **through** you.

> *How do you feel about that statement that God's love is FOR you?*

*What God says about Himself*

**Read Exodus 20:6 and 34:5-6.**

**What does God declare about Himself?**

The word often translated "lovingkindness" means a loyal love. The Bible clearly declares that God is love. And God's love is described as a loyal love.

**Read John 13:34-35.**

**What does Jesus as God's Son say about His love?**

Jesus, as God's Son, also declared love as part of His character and demonstrated that He loved those who followed Him.

*What others recognized about God's love*

**Read Psalm 103:8.**

**What descriptions are associated with God's love?**

The NET Bible says that God "demonstrates great loyal love." The Message translation uses the phrase "rich in love" to describe God's love.

**What comes to mind when you think of God "abounding in love" or "rich in love?"**

*Is that the way you walk around thinking about God?*

## God demonstrates His love.

Love is hard to define, but we can look at what God does to see what it looks like when He loves someone.

**Read 1 John 4:7-12.**

*How did God demonstrate His love for us (verse 9)?*

*What is characteristic of people who love God (verse 7)?*

*Why can we do this (verses 11-12)?*

**Read Romans 5:8.**

*How did God demonstrate His love for us?*

**Read Ephesians 2:4-5.**

*Because of God's great love for us, what did He also do?*

**Read Ephesians 3:17-19.**

*What did Paul pray for believers to be (verse 17)?*

*What did Paul want believers to grasp and know about God's love (verses 18-19)?*

You are dearly loved. God wants you to know this with confidence.

**Read Romans 8:38-39.**

*What can separate us from God's love?*

*So what is true about God's love for you?*

God's love is perfect. His love never changes. His love doesn't end. It is so vast that it never runs out. God doesn't stop loving. And nothing can ever separate you from God's love—not even you. Isn't that good to know?

Although we may feel love as an emotion, love is really a choice. God chose to love us, not because of anything we have done, or will do, but simply as a choice of His grace toward us.

*Jesus modeled God's love*

Because God loves us, He wants us to choose to love others as He does. One of the best ways to see that is to look at Jesus' life.

This is what Jesus told His disciples, "Anyone who has seen me has seen God the Father." When we read the life of Jesus in the Bible, we see that Jesus is the walking, talking, visible picture of who God is, what He does, and how He loves. How God loves people. Jesus was saying to His followers, "Want to know how to love? Look at me. Stay focused on me."

**Read John 11:5.**

*What is said about Jesus' love?*

Jesus loved His friends—Martha, Mary, and Lazarus. Jesus had been with His disciples for 3 years, loving them as He was teaching them how to love others. Jesus gave a new command to His disciples the night before He died.

**Read John 13:34-35.**

*What is the new command?*

*If we obey this command, what message do we give to those watching our lives?*

Jesus loved His followers very much. Because Jesus was God, He demonstrated God's love to them and to us. We can see God's love clearly when we look at Jesus' life in Matthew, Mark, Luke and John and see how Jesus interacted with people. To learn how to love God's way, we need to stay focused on Jesus. Jesus shows us how much God loves us. By faith, you can look to Jesus and watch what He did as He lived each day on earth.

**God's love is patient, kind, forgiving, and considers what is best for the one being loved.**

**Read John 15:9-13.**

*How did Jesus demonstrate His love for us (verse 13)?*

## TRUSTING YOUR FATHER GOD'S LOVE

God demonstrated His love for us through His gift of His Son Jesus Christ and through His death and resurrection. That's what we needed to overcome our greatest problem—our sin and the penalty of death that it brought to us. Through Jesus' death, we can be forgiven of all sin and enter a permanent loving relationship with our God. Through Jesus' resurrection, we can be given spiritual life beginning now and lasting forever.

> "Jesus Christ gave His life for you so He could give His life to you so He could live His life through you." (Ian Thomas, *The Saving Life of Christ*)

**Read Ephesians 5:1.**

*As a believer in Christ, what are you now called?*

*What difference does it make in your life to know you are dearly loved by your Father God?*

*Are you willing to trust His love for you?*

## DEEPER DISCOVERIES (OPTIONAL):

Spend a few minutes reading and reflecting on the following verses that reveal the "love" of God and why you can trust Him.

**Read Mark 5:1-43. Reflect on how Jesus demonstrated God's love to the demon-possessed man, the sick woman, the parents of the sick girl, and the sick girl herself.**

Read 1 Corinthians 13:4-8. This is a synopsis of God's love. Reflect on what you read, substituting "God's love" whenever you see the word "love."

Read John 17. Reflect on how Jesus' prayer demonstrates His love for us.

# 8: God's Joy

Trusting Your
Father God

*"The **joy** of the Lord makes you strong.*
*(Nehemiah 8:10 NIRV)*

> **Pray:** Lord Jesus, please teach me through this lesson.

## THE GOD YOU CAN KNOW

✓ God's SOVEREIGNTY: God is the sovereign ruler of His creation. He rules it with supreme authority and power.

✓ God's OMNIPOTENCE, OMNIPRESENCE, & OMNISCIENCE (the Omnis): God's power is more powerful than anything or anyone else in the entire universe. God's presence is everywhere at the same time. God knows everything there is to know.

✓ God's HOLINESS: God is holy. He is set apart from anything that is sinful or evil.

✓ God's JUSTICE: God always does what is morally right and fair.

✓ God's GRACE: God's grace is His undeserved favor abundantly poured out on those who desperately need Him.

✓ God's GOODNESS: God is good all the time — even in the tough times, in different ways for each person, and in what He allows or doesn't allow into our lives.

✓ God's LOVE: God's love is patient, kind, forgiving and considers what is best for the one being loved.

## ATTRIBUTE #8: JOY

Today, our lesson is about God's JOY.

**When you hear the word "joy," what comes to mind?**

Most people define joy as a feeling of happiness when you are smiling and laughing a lot. And they think that happiness comes from "good happenings." Good happenings mean everything is going your way, turning out right. You have lots of money and are healthy and are very successful in work or school. Right?

But what happens if things are not so good? Your family is stressed financially. You may be struggling in work or school. Your relationships are fraying. You or someone close to you is very sick. Can you really have joy then?

In the Bible, joy is a **deep inner gladness regardless of circumstances** going on around you. That means whether you are rich or poor, sick or healthy, successful or struggling, you can still have a feeling of gladness or pleasure deep down inside. Now, you may not feel like smiling on the outside, but you can still smile on the inside. Have you ever felt that way?

This kind of joy that I am describing is supernatural. It is part of the character of God and comes to us only from a relationship with Him through knowing Jesus Christ.

*What God says about Himself*

**Read Luke 15:1-7.**

*Who is rejoicing and why (verse 6)?*

*Who is rejoicing and why (verse 7)?*

**Read Luke 15:8-10.**

*Who is rejoicing and why (verse 9)?*

*Who is rejoicing and why (verse 10)?*

In both stories, something was lost, sought after, and found. Those on earth rejoice with the shepherd who finds a lost sheep and with the woman who finds her lost money. Likewise, God has joy whenever anyone comes to Him to have his or her sins forgiven. He is the one rejoicing along with the angels (verse 10).

The Bible also teaches that God finds great pleasure in His creation. Do you remember what God said about His creation at the end of each of the creation days? He said it was good. After day 6, He said it was very good. God wasn't only giving His approval but was also revealing His pleasure. The Father God has joy in what His hands have made, especially His creatures. That includes you. You are one of His creatures.

## What others recognized about God's joy

**Read 1 Timothy 1:11.**

*How did Paul describe God?*

The word "blessed" used here by Paul can also be translated "happy." So you can read the verse as "glorious good news of the happy God." The glorious good news is the gospel—how we can trust in Jesus and receive God's grace and forgiveness for our sins. God is happy, you could say He is joyful, to offer this good news to people. Our God is a joyful God.

In the lesson about God's grace (Lesson 5), you saw Jesus teaching that our Father God was like the father of the prodigal son when he returned home. Do you remember how that father acted? He was happy to see his son, filled with love, running toward him, hugging and kissing him. He called for a great celebration. That's joy.

**Read Zephaniah 3:17.**

Knowing God is with you and is mighty to save is wonderful confidence.

*What else does God do that expresses His emotions for you as one of His own?*

To take great delight (NIV) means to rejoice and display joy. God is rejoicing over you with gladness and singing because of your faith in His Son.

*Have you ever thought about God taking great delight in you? How does knowing that make you feel?*

*How does knowing that God rejoices over you with singing affect you?*

God's joy finds great pleasure in His creation and His creatures, especially people who trust in Him.

*God gives joy.*

Joy is something that God has. But it's also something that God gives. He is the source of joy, just as He is the source of love and grace as we have already studied. Jesus told His disciples about this gift of joy.

**Read John 15:11.**

*What does Jesus give to those who trust in Him?*

*Why?*

Jesus, who was God, had God's joy **in** Him. And He promised to give His joy to His disciples so that it would be **in** them, also. Jesus didn't promise this to just those who knew Him when He was on earth.

**Read 1 Peter 1:8.**

*What did Peter write to you who believe in Christ now?*

*How did Peter describe the joy God gives to you?*

Though you have not seen Him, the moment you believe in Jesus Christ, the Holy Spirit comes to live inside of you. And He gives you God's glorious, uncontainable joy.

There's a song you may have sung that says, "The joy of the Lord is my strength." That phrase comes from the book of Nehemiah in the Old Testament.

**Read Nehemiah 8:10.**

*What does God's joy do for you?*

*If God's joy is the ability to smile on the inside even if things are going wrong on the outside, how could having that make you strong?*

I have had a sign on my wall for over 40 years that reads, "Joy is the most infallible sign of the presence of God." That continually reinforces my faith because even during the tough times I have felt the joy of the Lord giving me strength. It is during those miserable, painful times that God's joy inside of us assures us of His presence with us. Don't you love that assurance?!

The joy of the Lord is God's joy. He has it, and when He gives it to His people, it makes them strong. God's joy in us gives us the courage to face tough times. **God's joy finds great pleasure in His creation and His creatures, especially people who trust in Him.** His joy in us makes us strong.

## TRUSTING YOUR FATHER GOD'S JOY

God is a God of joy. He rejoices in His creation, and He rejoices in the salvation of lost sinners. As His dearly loved child, then you can be in tune with the heart and character of God and should thus be characterized by joy as well.

*Having God's joy in us, we should delight in the things in which God delights. We can ask ourselves: "What delights God? What gives Him joy?" How would you answer that?*

When you have His joy, then you should take pleasure or delight in those same things. When you have the joy of the Lord, you rejoice in justice. You find pleasure in God and knowing Him, not in personal and selfish pleasures. You also find delight in studying His word (the Bible), in doing what pleases Him, and in praising God.

Some people think that when you are a Christian, you give up anything that gives you pleasure. That is not what the Bible says. It is not wrong for a Christian to have pleasure or to seek pleasure. It is only wrong to seek pleasure in the things that are selfish.

Christians filled with God's joy should find many reasons to laugh and delight in life. We can serve God with delight. We can praise God and sing worship songs with delight. We can love our families and friends with delight. We can do our work with delight. And our joy will be even greater in heaven when we are with Jesus and can have the delight of seeing Him with our own eyes.

Your Father God gives you freedom to enjoy life whether or not everything is going your way.

**Read and reflect on the following quote:**

"There is no joy like that of knowing God and serving Him, no joy like that of knowing that our sins are forgiven and we are right with God through the shed blood of Jesus Christ. There is no joy that endures pain and suffering and persecution like the joy of the Christian, whose hope and joy are in the Lord, and not in our circumstances." (Robert Deffinbaugh, "Let Me See Thy Glory: A Study of the Attributes of God," p. 137, posted on Bible.org)

*Feel free to use any means to express the joy of the Lord in your life.*

*Praise your Father God for who He is and for being a joyful God. Thank Him for finding pleasure in His creation and in His children, including you. Ask Him to help you find pleasure in knowing Him.*

## DEEPER DISCOVERIES (OPTIONAL):

Spend a few minutes reading and reflecting on the following verses that reveal the "joy" of God and why you can trust Him.

**Read Acts 4:23-35. Reflect on the joy of the Lord experienced by the disciples.**

**Read Philippians 1:3-26. Reflect on the joy of the Lord experienced by Paul and how he encouraged others to experience God's joy as well.**

# Resources

1. Ian Thomas, The Saving Life of Christ

2. John Newton, Amazing Grace lyrics

3. John Piper, desiringgod.org, posted on March 8, 2016

4. R. C. Sproul, The Holiness of God

5. Reagan Rodgers, "Silver Linings"

6. Reginald Heber, Holy, Holy, Holy Lord God Almighty" lyrics

7. Robert Deffinbaugh, "Let Me See They Glory: A Study of the Attributes of God," posted on Bible.org

8. William McDowell, "You Are God Alone" lyrics)

www.ingramcontent.com/pod-product-compliance
Lightning Source LLC
Chambersburg PA
CBHW061712120626
46550CB00003B/1201